HAWKE'S BAY IN COLOUR

FRONTISPIECE Dawn over the sea at Napier.
Sun rises, day follows night, ebb follows flow . . . constant in a changing world.

HAWKE'S BAY
IN COLOUR

Text by KAY MOONEY

A. H. & A. W. REED

WELLINGTON SYDNEY LONDON

First published 1975

A. H. & A. W. REED LTD

182 Wakefield Street, Wellington
53 Myoora Road, Terrey Hills, Sydney 2084
11 Southampton Row, London WC1B 5HA

also

16–18 Beresford Street, Auckland
165 Cashel Street, Christchurch

© 1975 KAY MOONEY
ISBN 0 589 00942 7

Printed and bound by
Kyodo Printing Company Ltd. Tokyo

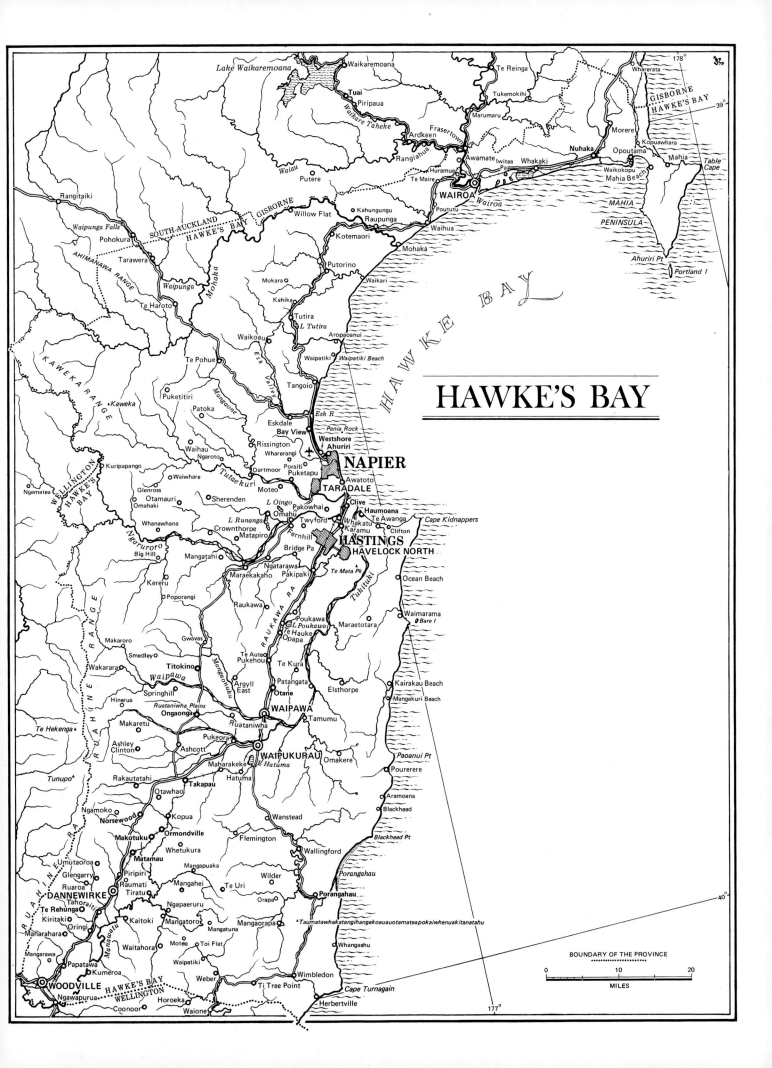

HAWKE'S BAY

INTRODUCTION

Hawke's bay was settled by Europeans in a haphazard way; no organised settlement, this, to a carefully thought-out plan of colonisation—just the back end of Wellington province to which only the more daring, enterprising or desperate settlers would go.

By the time Hawke's Bay became a self-governing province it was made up of all types and classes, tough, tenacious, daring people who made a province powerful politically and economically. Their differences were their strengths; they knew this and they made use of the knowledge.

In our day it is usually only in football that the provinces of New Zealand become vibrantly aware of their separate provincial identities. Outside this sphere, ubiquity is cultivated as a virtue. To be different is to be suspect.

This attitude is compounded by good transport services, a footloose population ready to change jobs and change towns at short notice, generous holidays and fast-moving holiday habits. Populations change and exchange with bewildering rapidity and not many people can say with conviction that they belong on this spot of New Zealand or that.

One group can say this; Maori people have retained the awareness that a particular communal strength comes of knowing exactly where one's roots go down, the place from which one draws identity and dignity and confidence. In recent years Europeans have begun to sense something missing in their foothold on the land on which they live. They have begun to look for their roots. This is something the pioneer generation could not pass down to their children, something they never had themselves. And so, transport and communication and happy feet notwithstanding, a new provincialism is emerging, the first step towards a new nationalism.

When we look into these pictures, we look into Hawke's Bay. Every photograph is a time aperture, a piece of the present but the present is only the piece of the iceberg that shows above the water. The past lies just below the surface and so does the future.

Some of these beautiful and tranquil scenes conceal a past of violence and greed when man outraged nature and regarded the land beneath his feet as a commodity to be exploited; an earlier past when man preyed upon man in tribal warfare; an even earlier period in the dreamtime of New Zealand when terrible natural forces heaved and boiled and tore the land from the bed of the ocean, threw up its mountain ranges, carved its river gorges.

Behind the rolling pastures and the fat, placid sheep, the sunny orchards and the fruitful vines, the shopping mall, the car-park and the golf club, is a growing realisation that the one who draws life and sustenance from this land is drinking from a deep fountain. He is putting down his roots into soil of which he knows little, being shaped by forces beyond his comprehension.

Sometimes the very old come to know this, sometimes the young are able to sense it. But there are many confused people in the middle who rely on television to pinpoint their needs and changing one's toothpaste or shampoo doesn't seem to achieve much for them.

Yet the Maori neighbour goes home to his family place to a funeral and his toes take a grip on the ground there and he knows himself and he is strong again.

Hawke's Bay, from its ragged start, exhibited a certain raw energy and determination although this was sometimes masked by an appearance of pastoral peacefulness. It mixed social awareness and rude vitality, opportunism and idealism. Its first settlers were people who knew what they wanted and saw to it that they got it . . . flourishing businesses, fertile farms, prosperous towns.

Hawke's Bay people of today are just realising that if they want to keep and enjoy the good things so plentifully given to them they are going to have to be just as firm and ruthless and determined in their effort to repair the damages done by greed and ignorance, to prevent a repetition of the mistakes of the past, to learn to know themselves in unity with the land on which they stand.

In these pictures of Hawke's Bay today in its varying beauty may be seen echoes of the past, hints about the future, strands in a design yet to be completed.

CAPTAIN COOK sailed across this stretch of Hawke's Bay more than two hundred years ago and he recorded what he saw . . . the bluff head, the stony beach, the snow mountains in the distance.

Dumont D'Urville, the French explorer, sailed past fifty years after Cook and he recorded that in all New Zealand this part was without doubt the richest and most attractive offered to his gaze.

Centuries before the sails of the two explorers came up over the horizon the canoes from Polynesia had swept in through the long breakers and into the shelter of the bluff head. The canoe people laid claim to the swamp and the lagoon and the bush on the hills, the teeming food supply from river, sea, swamp and land. This foodbasket was the envy of other tribes and they had to fight so hard to defend it that the name of the foreshore was Upoko Poiti—floating heads, heads floating in the tide.

Later the whalers came and the beaches were stained with oil and blood as commerce took its hold.

Then the settlers came with their bonneted wives and numerous children and after them came the clergyman and the brewer, the butcher, the baker, the stay-maker and the candlestick-maker.

And the chiefs' names, once placed on the land as a tapu to make it inviolate, gave way to European names redolent of imperial victory and colonial success.

A century passed; flowers bloomed and grass gleamed, trees grew, meticulously spaced, and electric lights appeared in their branches; fountains played in many colours.

Holiday visitors came in large numbers and, like the canoe people before them, like Cook and D'Urville, they liked what they saw.

The endless shingle spit, the oil-stained strand, the fought-over food basket of the tribes, had been turned into fairyland . . . or so it seemed.

PLATE 1   The City of Napier at twilight, looking south along the Marine Parade.

NAPIER is a pleasant and sunny holiday town and when the holidaymakers throng the golden mile of Marine Parade it is easy to believe that the city has no other aim than to provide entertainment and accommodation, to guarantee unrivalled sunshine and a happy holiday.

In fact, Napier is a tough and determined town—servicing centre for a prosperous rural area, an important port, the largest wool centre in the North Island, the base for numerous industries.

At the start of settlement few people would have cared to bet on Napier's chance of developing into a large city but, in spite of gloomy prospects, it did grow. It grew over every piece of dry land and into the most impossible crevices of the hill. And when it had grown over all these, it drained blocks of swampy lagoon and built out on to that.

1931 brought a grim setback. The earthquake in that year practically wiped out the town but it rose from the ashes and kept on growing. This time it had 7500 acres of new land thrown up by the earthquake when the bed of the sea was raised and its growth from this time on was spectacular.

The wreckage and rubble of old Napier was used to lay a foundation for the Marine Parade Gardens, centre of the holiday area. On a plaque in the Gardens, these words are inscribed:

I never understood how man could dare
To feel the tremors, hear the tragic sound
Of houses twisting, crushing, everywhere
And not be conquered by a sick despair.
Although his buildings crumble to a mound
Of worthless ruins, man has always found
The urge to build a stronger city there.
Within my soul I made my towers high,
They lie in ruins yet I have begun
To build again, now planning to restore
What life has shaken to the earth, and I
In faith shall build my towers towards the sun,
A stronger city than was there before.

PLATE 2   The ocean beach at Napier (*top*)
An aerial view of Napier (*lower*)

THE HARBOUR at Napier serves the whole of the eastern and central areas of the North Island. It handles more than a million tons of cargo a year and this includes fertilisers, petroleum products, cement, logs, woodpulp, frozen meat, fruit and wool.

Harbour history in Napier is an enthralling story of century-long guerilla warfare and political manoeuvring with one party supporting the development of an inner harbour in the smooth water behind the hill while the other favoured an outer harbour protected from the open sea by a concrete block wall.

One argued—and fought to support the argument—that it would be impossible to dredge a channel deep enough to serve a harbour in behind the hill; the other thought it would be impossible to build a sea-wall strong enough and long enough to keep the Pacific out of an outer harbour.

Finally, the breakwater party won, much helped by the 1931 earthquake which lifted the sea-bed and more or less put the inner harbour out of commission for deep-sea shipping.

The sea-wall was built and today protects shipping carrying trade of a volume and diversity never imagined in the fighting days of the great controversy.

The port of Napier will soon provide improved weather protection, land reclamation for pre-assembly facilities to deal with the changing techniques of cargo handling associated with the newer designs in ships.

PLATE 3   The Port of Napier from Bluff Hill

Now it is known as the Centennial Gardens, a place of beauty and peace with a seventy-three foot waterfall splashing down the cliff face into a flower-bordered pool, showering with spray the visitors and their cameras.

But previously this has been an unhappy place. Until a few years ago it was the prison quarry. On its stark face prisoners from Napier gaol worked to lever out rocks and boulders and send them crashing to the quarry floor below where fellow-prisoners armed with pick-axes and sledge-hammers broke them up into manageable quarry stone.

From the stone were made the hill roads of Napier and the many retaining walls that hold together the patchwork gardens of the homes built into the folds and crevices of the hill.

A hundred years ago this was the site of the Pauper's Refuge, a grim building into which were herded the misfits of colonial society—drunkards, the feeble-minded, unmarried maternity cases, destitute terminal illness patients.

On the other side of the hill was the prison and the place where executions by hanging took place. Further up the hill were the cells that served as a lunatic asylum.

In centuries before this was a sacred spot, the place at which the first fruits of the season were offered up, a spot too sacred for the feet of ordinary men.

Over the years this has been an area darkened by ritual sacrifice, suffering and despair.

Now it is a place of flowers and fountains and laughter, symbol of beauty and regeneration, symbol of Napier turning with hope and imagination into its second century as a town.

PLATE 4   The waterfall in the Centennial Gardens at
Napier

T HIS PHOTOGRAPH, looking down Hastings Street from the foot of Shakespeare Road, is taken from a spot of considerable interest in the history of Hawke's Bay. This was the site of the Provincial Council Chamber when Hawke's Bay was a self-governing province.

In the early 1850s, New Zealand consisted of six provinces. Because there was little communication between them—no roads and not much coastal shipping—they were like six independent colonies. In 1858, Hawke's Bay petitioned to be separated from Wellington and it celebrated its independence with a public dinner, a ball and two days' racing.

From this date until 1876, the Hawke's Bay Provincial Council was responsible for making its own legislation to deal with matters of land-buying, immigration, public works, roads and bridges and harbour planning, education and hospital.

Within the little wooden parliament building with picket fence outside, a full ceremonial in the best Westminster tradition was carried out. Mr Speaker was in control and the mace was solemnly carried in and laid down before business started. The Hon. Members, when they stepped out from their legislative chamber, stood just about where the photographer stood to take this photograph but they looked down a very different Hastings Street. They saw single-storey wooden shops, some with false frontage to make them look two-storey, no pavements, an unmade road which was a dust-trap in summer and a sea of mud in winter, hacks tied up to posts, buggies, drays, water-carts.

But the business of Napier was going on. Some of today's big commercial concerns were getting their start.

These houses on Marine Parade, Napier, are a fine example of the better type of home that was being built in the 1870s and 1880s when the pioneering period was finished and the settlement and development period was in full swing.

It is the policy of the City Council to develop the Parade for residential and accommodation buildings. This permits apartment houses, hotels and motels and it is anticipated that there will be an increase in the number of high-rise buildings.

The Council, however, is encouraging the preservation of the better old houses in order to retain something of the gracious flavour of old Napier when the only entertainment available on the Parade was a band concert in the band rotunda.

PLATE 5   Gardens in Hastings Street, Napier (*top*)
Homes on the Marine Parade, Napier (*lower*)

TE MATA is the dominant peak of the hills behind Havelock North, an area rich in Maori history and tradition. In earlier centuries when Rongokako the giant ranged there, Te Mata looked down over a very different landscape where the Tukituki River wandered at will, changing and rechanging its bed, depositing its load of silt and building up the land.

The Tukituki drains the eastern side of the Ruahine Range and it formed the Ruataniwha plains of central Hawke's Bay by deposition of the spoil it carried down from the ranges.

The Tukituki was a regular river highway for both Maori and European and the story of many of the central Hawke's Bay and coastal stations starts with a family making a frightening journey up the Tukituki to take up their land, to burn off the fern, sow grass seed into the ashes, turn hungry sheep on to the blackened ground to eat every new fern frond as it appeared, to grow their wool and send it back downriver to market.

Whale boats, Maori canoes and large unwieldy punts did a brisk business in river traffic for many years and the settlers learned a hard lesson from the hardship and economic burden of unsatisfactory transport. The ingenuity they acquired to deal with that problem is being applied today to other problems.

Nearly three quarters of New Zealand is today sheep country and meat and wool provide half of the country's export income so it is small wonder that much time and finance are put into trying to breed better sheep, grow better pastures, develop better methods of marketing and managing.

New Zealand was one of the first countries to undertake top-dressing from the air and many farms in Hawke's Bay have benefited from this method. Bulldozers have been used to cut roads into steep hillsides so that the jeep may replace the horse. Motorcycles have come into use for mustering and shepherds' dogs have learned to ride pillion with remarkable aplomb.

In spite of this, the man on the horse at the back of a mob of sheep is a familiar sight and any who attend sheep dog trials will agree that they have not yet found a replacement for a good dog.

PLATE 6   A pastoral view overlooking the Tukituki River near Havelock North

THEY LOOKED for gold in Hawke's Bay in the early days. They looked in the rivers and the mountain creeks, they prospected in the ranges and they finally came to realise that the real gold of Hawke's Bay was quietly grazing in the paddocks all the time.

Today there are six million sheep in Hawke's Bay—give or take a few. On the higher hill country towards the ranges the sheep get on with their part in the meat and wool business, the breeding. On the good land of the flats the animals are fattened. In between on the easier hill country there is an intermediate system of both breeding and fattening.

So for some it is business as usual on the high country, for others it is a quick ride down the road to the meat works if they are lucky, a slow walk if they are not, and the doubtful glory of representing Hawke's Bay on the tables of the mutton- and lamb-eaters of the world.

And between them they also produce two-and-a-half million dollars worth of wool per year.

There is only one-tenth as many cattle in the province as there are sheep—600,000. They also tend to be bred in the higher rainfall areas and fattened on the fertile flats.

Although Hawke's Bay in general is not a dairying area, the dairy cow plays an important part in the productivity of the southern part of the district.

Cattle breeding is an active and enterprising branch of the business and a strong interest has recently been shown in the introduction of new breeds to New Zealand. Angus and Herefords, the mainstay, are now being used to build up new breeds from imported semen. . . . Charolais, Simmental, Limousin.

Both the sheep farmer and the cow farmer look at the spiral of rising farm costs, the need for new machines, new management systems; they look at research work in progress with promise of an increase in production and they grimly hope that the latter will keep them ahead of the former.

And in the meantime, the rain falls, the sun shines and the grass grows and flocks and herds increase themselves obediently and then join the procession down the road.

And that's the story of sheep and cattle anywhere.

PLATE 7   Docking sheep at Ruakawa in Central Hawke's Bay (*top*)
Cattle grazing at Putorino (*lower*)

THE VISITOR to New Zealand finds it almost impossible to get away from sheep. Sheep litter the landscape. Every hill is dotted with white specks, every paddock being grazed.

Sixty million sheep in the country and three million people, that's twenty each murmurs the tourist as his luxury coach slides through the countryside. This, as the poet said and the bus driver repeats, is a country where the sheep is king.

The musterers and their dogs on the hills and the obedient lines of sheep ambling one behind the other towards the yards are the start of a chain of processes and transactions leading to overseas merchant houses and manufacturers throughout the world, to many people wearing New Zealand wool as fashion as well as for warmth, to many feet treading New Zealand carpet.

The production and export of wool and the safeguarding of the national wool income is a nerve-wracking see-saw of a business. The amount rung up on the cash registers of the shops in the towns and cities of Hawke's Bay bears a direct relationship to the financial situation of the man on the land.

The sheep is king indeed.

Wool has had its bad days in recent years and the town economy has staggered with each new blow to the wool trade. One of the darkest of threats came from the increase in man-made fibres. However, there is considerable optimism in the wool business as the threat from synthetics has lessened and increased demand for wool indicates that it has become a prestige fibre as well as a useful one.

Wool, it is realised, does not require the use of petro-chemicals for its production and man-made fibres do. Wool grows because grass grows and grass needs solar energy to make it grow.

And if there is one thing Hawke's Bay has been blessed with it is plenty of sunshine and adequate rain.

PLATE 8   Mustering sheep along the shores of Lake Runanga

UNTIL the end of the 19th century, Hawke's Bay was a province of very large sheep runs. Then a bloodless revolution broke the large estates into smaller blocks and ushered in an era of more intensive farming.

Before the days of refrigerated shipping in the 1880s, sheep were bred solely for wool and their meat was a by-product hard to get rid of. With the coming of refrigeration and the opening of a European market, a revolution in sheep breeding started, an effort to develop a good sheep meat or, even better, a sheep good for meat and wool.

The first sheepfarmers in Hawke's Bay had no advisory body, no research station to help them. They imported good stud stock and worked on a process of trial and error. Some strange theories about the science of breeding were current at this time. Some people feared that mutton from merino sheep was unsafe to eat because it might inflame the passions. A learned judge, sitting in the Supreme Court in Napier in the 1880s, attributed the increase in crime in Hawke's Bay to the giving up of merino meat in favour of the coarser Lincoln mutton. Others expressed grave doubts about the effect on the moral fibre of New Zealanders of a diet of Romney mutton, the Romney having been originally bred on bleak salt marshes.

Today, sheepfarmers and their advisers are still experimenting with an eye to the markets of the future. The farmer works against rising costs of land and labour and he cannot afford to farm any animals not producing well in two basic ways—their weight of wool and their fertility.

Among the new breeds of sheep developed to meet the challenge of the day are the Coopworth, a cross of Border Leicester over Romney, and the Perendale, a Cheviot over Romney cross. By a process of cross-breeding and then inter-breeding, these new breeds have been established and promise well.

The Coopworth is both fertile and a good wool producer and although it can survive in most parts of New Zealand it does best on good country. The Perendale is more suited to higher and harder country. It grows fine wool and less wool and so can survive and produce under harder conditions.

One advantage of both these new breeds is that they can look after themselves at lambing time and do not need a shepherd-midwife. It is good farming business when neither the sheep nor the farmer has a serious labour problem.

PLATE 9   Shepherd mustering sheep (*top*)
Droving sheep along a Hawke's Bay road (*lower*)

THERE is no problem of lack of mechanisation in the hay-making business these days. The main difficulty here is to synchronise the availability of the machines with the suitability of the weather.

A large amount of hay is grown on the Ruataniwha plains. It is baled and stacked on contract and the big difficulty is that every farm wants the machines in at the same time and the weather has a habit of deteriorating as soon as one's turn arrives.

Hay is cut and left to dry, then turned and tossed by discs to hasten the process. When it is dry, the mechanical baler moves along the rows; it gobbles up loose hay and puts out finished bundles to be collected by men with trucks and taken to the haybarns.

As soon as it is safely in the barn the farmer can breathe again and he doesn't mind how dark the sky grows.

But it was not always like this. The New Zealand farmer, because of the nature of the land, has been forced to develop a mechanical mind. He suffered from a shortage of manpower and he tried to overcome this as best he could by producing a large family. He frequently suffered from isolation from his neighbours and had no friend to help in an emergency. He was almost always some distance from the sources of supply.

So he improvised and invented. He used what materials he had to hand with a great deal of ingenuity. New Zealand has a fine record for invention and resourcefulness, for improving methods and machines and using them productively.

Horse-drawn mowers, rakes and hay-sweeps were in use at an early date. Hay grabs and stackers were also operated by horses. The giant machines of today, moving inexorably over the paddocks about their business, make harvesting a matter of booking a day and paying the account. But one thing remains unchanged ... the farmer feels the same panic when his hay is lying out to dry and big black rain clouds fill the sky.

PLATE 10 Haybaling at Waipawa

STACKING is a dying craft. There are few people left in New Zealand—land of highly-mechanised farming—who could make stacks like those seen in the picture.

They were the work of a Maori farmer who lives at Omahu, a few miles out of Hastings, and he was taught by his father.

Omahu is a Maori settlement rich in pre-European history. The hill-slopes and fertile areas on the banks of river and stream and lake were places rich in food and so this was an area closely-settled by Maori people. There were abundant eels and freshwater mussels, generous growth of fern-root and kumara, birds in the swamps and in the bush.

Because it was such a garden of food, it was much coveted and, in the centuries before the Europeans arrived, it was the scene of many tribal fights. Raids on a neighbour's eel weirs and plantations were the sporting fixture of the day and a man who proved himself brave and cunning and resourceful could expect the respect of his people and the best of the women. The chief of this area in later years refused all offers of honours and titles from Queen and Government because, he said, nothing could exceed the mana he had from being leader of his own people.

Inherited knowledge has always been passed from father to son in this area but the art of stacking was learned from no Maori forebear. An English stacker who was concerned that the craft would die with his generation was eager to pass it on, and so a traditional skill of the English country-side came to a part of Hawke's Bay where tradition is valued.

A row of a dozen stacks with twelve tons of oats in each is a satisfactory harvest but there is no easy way with this crop, no machines to make the work easier. Both stacking and stooking take manpower and time as well as skill. Delivery becomes an expensive business when the customers may be more than a hundred miles away.

So the stackers decide to forget the horse and its needs and become cow farmers.

And this may be the last picture of oat stacks taken in Hawke's Bay.

PLATE 11   Oat stacks at Omahu on the banks of the Ngaruroro River (*top*)
Sheaves of oats placed in stocks to ripen and dry out before stacking at Omahu (*lower*)

A JOY in springtime in its bright new foliage, a pleasure to see in autumn when the leaves are turning, Oak Avenue can look just as striking in winter when its canopy of bare branches allows the winter sun to filter through.

The mile-long stand of oaks is considered the finest avenue of large trees in New Zealand. It has passed its century of life and in December 1974, a bronze plaque was erected in the avenue to mark the fact.

Originally Oak Avenue was the tree-lined drive to Karamu homestead. Karamu was one of the sections of Heretaunga block, the heart of the plains. When first leased for settlement it was a raupo swamp but within a few years it was described as the richest and fattest land on the plains. Its story is typical of the planning and enthusiasm and knowledge—to say nothing of the capital—poured into the establishing of the great Hawke's Bay estates.

Tree-planting on the grand scale was part of the master plan—tree-planting to conserve the land, to provide shade and browse, to attract the rain, to trap the silt of flooded rivers but also for the sheer beauty of a fine tree.

Karamu station had, when the homestead was built in 1874, twelve plantations of trees and imported birds such as the blackbird were released into them. Young trees were raised in conservatories. . . . Australian light trees for practical use, willow, poplar and pine for quick-growing shelter belts, ornamental shrubs of all descriptions for the house gardens, fruit trees of every kind for the domestic orchards, oaks to lay out an imposing driveway up to the mansion.

The great estates have long since been reduced into many smaller properties and Oak Avenue is now a public road but it is surely the best memorial the original settler could have asked to the fact that he passed this way, for a time he owned the land and he beautified it with noble trees.

PLATE 12   Oak Avenue, Hastings

FRIMLEY was another of the large estates acquired by an ambitious settler when Heretaunga block was leased for settlement. Its owner, too, was a dedicated tree-planter. The part now Frimley Park has, fittingly, been given to the people of Hastings as a public reserve.

The park contains some beautiful and historic trees. One of these, a necklace poplar, planted in 1875, is, at 145 feet, recorded as the largest deciduous tree in New Zealand and one of the largest poplars in the world.

Although the magnificence of Frimley today lies in its trees, it has another claim to fame. Both local government for Hastings and the chief industry of the area had their start in the historic Frimley wool shed.

The first meeting of settlers to impose a rate upon themselves and build the first road was held in Frimley woolshed before the name Hastings had been heard of. It was the conversion of the woolshed into a canning factory that began the march of the district towards the vast fruit-growing and food-processing industry of the present.

The beauty of Cornwall Park also lies in its mature trees and in its streams and pools of water. It also has aviaries of exotic birds and common birds and a display house for seasonal hothouse flowers.

This park is the propagating nursery and from it plants are taken out to the many flower beds which have been laid out to add colour and beauty to the inner city area.

Cornwall Park is the cricketing headquarters of Hastings and this sport also is made more pleasurable by a setting among fine shady trees.

PLATE 13   The Rose Garden in Frimley Park (*top*)
Cornwall Park, Hastings (*lower*)

ORIGINALLY it was a barren swamp regularly inundated by the Ngaruroro River.

Then it was acquired for settlement from the Maori owners and it became a handful of large estates of several thousand acres each and the owners went to work to drain and plant and cultivate the land.

Next, two of the owners subdivided and many 100-acre properties came into being and these were even more intensively cultivated. And a small township, Karamu, was born to service the settlers and their properties.

Then the railway came through and the 100-acre farmers in their turn subdivided and they sold in lots as small as five acres. In no time houses and shops and businesses began to appear, streets were laid out, the hamlet of Karamu became the town of Hastings.

Hastings just grew and grew and it was only a very few years before it was challenging Napier for the role of capital city of Hawke's Bay and urging people engaged in business in Napier to quit the hills which were fast becoming so crowded and come to Hastings to enjoy the advantages and pleasures of living on the plains.

Today it is one of New Zealand's most rapidly-developing provincial areas and its urban population exceeds that of Napier. It is a city with a mild climate, plenty of employment available, prosperous people; a place of fine old trees and pleasant homes set in beautiful gardens.

In recent years a determined effort has been made to create a restful atmosphere in a busy city teeming with commercial life. This has been achieved by allowing no through traffic in the main shopping areas, by pavements treated to muffle the sound of footsteps, by intersections bright with flowers and seats in shady corners.

Hastings is the servicing, banking and commercial centre for one of the richest rural areas of New Zealand and the heart of a vast complex of food-processing factories, meat-freezing works, cool-stores, dairy factories and wine-makers—the outlets for the products of the area.

PLATE 14   Heretaunga Street, Hastings (*top*)
A view looking over Havelock North to
Hastings in the distance (*lower*)

THE DEVELOPMENT of the Heretaunga Plains into the agricultural heart of Hawke's Bay is one of the more spectacular episodes in the history of the province.

With its fertile alluvial soil, plentiful artesian water, moderate rainfall and high sunshine hours, the plains area is ideally suited to fruitgrowing.

F. W. Sturm, son of a gardener at the Imperial Palace in Vienna, was probably Hawke's Bay's first apple grower. Sturm traded not in fruit but in trees and he found ready buyers for his stock. Settlers who planted apple trees in their gardens and domestic orchards were not thinking in terms of new industries. They looked for a supply of fresh fruit for the table and the kitchen, a shade to sit under on hot summer days, apple blossom in springtime to bring tears of homesickness.

Towards the end of the century an increasing demand for fruit to meet the needs of a growing population led to the establishment of commercial orchards but, because of ignorance of disease control, their yield was low. With the establishment of the Department of Agriculture to instruct and advise, cool-store facilities to make marketing easier, and the Apple and Pear Marketing Board to bring some measure of financial security, apple growing in Hawke's Bay became big business.

After World War I, many new orchards were established by returned soldiers with Government assistance. This period saw the increase of small, owner-worked orchards. A ten-acre property with eight acres in fruit was considered a proposition by which a man could make a living if not a fortune.

In recent years new methods of orchard management have reduced much of the labour of commercial apple-growing. Picking into large bins or trailers, the use of speed sprayers, mechanical ladders, conveyor belts and elevators, even water dumping, have all made harvesting quicker and more profitable.

There is little processing of apples and the apple crop of Hawke's Bay finds its way to the markets of New Zealand and, as export fresh fruit, into the markets of the world.

PLATE 15   Apples for export (*top*)
Loading export apples at the Port of Napier (*lower*)

THERE WAS ONCE a woman from Hawke's Bay who went to Japan for a holiday. And everyone told her she must make her visit in fruit-blossom time for this, they said, was the most beautiful sight anyone could ever see.

So she did. And it was. And it was just like the sight she saw in every direction from the windows of her own home in Hawke's Bay in blossom time.

Even before the settlers came and planted their gardens and orchards, every Maori village had its grove of peach trees grown from peach-stones accepted as payment from flax-traders and whalers. Guns were the favoured currency at this period but peachstones made good small change.

Very early in the story of settlement it was seen that the peaches growing so abundantly could be made into a commercial proposition if only an economical method of drying or otherwise processing could be devised.

Housewives dried peaches and hung them up in strings like onions; they made peach leather and rolled it up like cardboard. But businessmen were hesitant about putting their investment capital into peaches until they could see a clearer path to the markets.

Finally, at the turn of the century, the Frimley Cannery was established. Machinery was imported, a woolshed was turned into a canning factory and sixty miles of peach trees were planted. There were sixty rows, each row a mile long, each row available for sale on terms to fruitgrowers who would have the security of the cannery as their outlet.

And so the fruit-processing industry of Hawke's Bay was started. Frimley lasted only a few years but it pointed the way for the giant food processing concerns of today.

An interesting side-issue of the fruit-picking and processing is the large amount of seasonal work available. Many degrees from all the universities of New Zealand have been financed by hard work in the hot Hawke's Bay sun during university vacations.

PLATE 16   Blossom time in Hawke's Bay (*top*)
Harvesting golden queen peaches at a
Hastings orchard (*lower*)

DEEP DEPOSITS of alluvial soil and bountiful supplies of artesian water make the Heretaunga Plains the richest cropping land in New Zeland.

Much of the cropping on the plains is contract growing for two major food-processing factories dealing in canned food and frozen food. Large acres of peas, beans, carrots, beet, tomatoes, asparagus, sweet corn, are grown for processing and for export to all parts of the Pacific basin and the United Kingdom.

Taradale lies in a sheltered position, warm and sunny, protected from the wind. Now it is a suburb of Napier but it still retains its identity and some of the atmosphere of a country town. It is a true mixed farming area and lamb-fattening, seed production, orcharding, vine-growing, market-gardening, process-cropping and dairying are all found in the district.

The tomato harvester seen in the photograph working near Hastings was the first of its type in New Zeland. It was imported from the United States by a food-processing company seeking a solution to the problem of insufficient labour available for hand picking. A person picking by hand is able to select the ripe fruit and make a second pick later but a machine moves relentlessly over the fields and gathers in everything, whether ripe or not.

The machine was imported earlier than had been thought possible because of research work carried out by the Department of Agriculture with ethrel, a chemical which accelerates the ripening of tomatoes and gives a higher proportion of red fruit ready for picking at a single harvest.

However, better varieties of tomato are needed to improve yields and spread the harvest over a longer period and the research facilities of private companies, universities and government departments are engaged in this work.

PLATE 17   Cultivation for cropping at Taradale (*top*)
Tomato harvesting near Hastings (*lower*)

MOUNT ST. MARY'S, on the slope of the hill at Green-meadows, is a seminary for the training of young men for the Catholic priesthood. Its vineyards produce the well-known Mission wine.

When the first Marists came to Hawke's Bay in 1850 they brought with them vine cuttings from stock brought out from France to ensure a supply of wine for the altar. Twenty years later the Government brought out to Hawke's Bay twelve families of vintners from the French wine country; they were to be settled on Mahia Peninsula to make rivers of wine flow.

Unfortunately this did not eventuate, but vineyards flourished in Havelock North, Taradale and the Esk Valley. Winegrowing reached a peak in the 1890s but it slumped in the early years of the new century when the abstinence crusade was making mighty progress. However, it rallied again and today is enjoying a boom as table wines become more popular in Hawke's Bay homes. About 1400 acres of the province is in vineyard and from this comes about three quarters of a million gallons per year. This is sold in all parts of New Zealand but the province retains and suitably accounts for a fair proportion of its wine.

And if wine-growing in Hawke's Bay owes a debt of gratitude to France, market-gardening owes one to China. Chinese settlers, frugal and efficient, have specialised in this form of farming and for many years they filled local needs and had a surplus to send to the markets of other North Island cities.

The Esk Valley lies to the north of the plains and opens up the route from plains and sea to the inland plateau and Lake Taupo. Ahuriri's first families of settlers chose it for themselves when what is now the fertile plain of Heretaunga was a raupo swamp.

Despite high productivity per acre, the market-gardener is always dependent upon two factors outside his control . . . the state of the market and the state of the weather. For this reason many market-gardeners are content to grow on contract for the food-processing factories.

However, there are still people who like their vegetables fresh from the earth and unprocessed. The gateway stall is prominent in Hawke's Bay and is still well patronised.

PLATE 18   The Mission Vineyards at Greenmeadows (*top*)
Market gardens at Eskdale (*lower*)

IT IS A STORY within a name and is claimed as the longest place name in the world—57 letters:

Taumatawhakatangihangakoauauotamateapokaiwhenua-kitanatahu

It means:

The summit of the hill on which Tamatea the traveller played the flute to his beloved.

This, surprisingly, is an abbreviated version. One phrase, referring to Tamatea's long legs pulling him up the mountain, has been dropped. The original name was:

Taumatawhakatangihangakoauauotamateapokaiwhenua-turipukakapikimaungahoronukukitanatahu.

85 letters, a record and a triumphant reply to the Welsh claimant for longest place name. The Welsh contender has a mere 58 letters in it and it is claimed that only the first twenty make up the official name.

Tamatea-pokai-whenua is one of the ancestral fathers of Hawke's Bay Maoris. He was the grandson of Tamatea-ariki-nui. Tamatea, the encircler of the earth, the great traveller, the grandson of Tamatea, the great chief. The elder Tamatea was captain of the canoe Takitimu from which the people of Hawke's Bay claim descent. He brought the sacred sea-going canoe from its Polynesian homeland to the islands of New Zealand.

The younger Tamatea built another canoe also called Takitimu and he made a voyage of exploration of the coast-line of New Zealand not only before Captain Cook did the same but before Christopher Columbus set off on his voyage of exploration.

The beloved to whom he played his flute on the hill-top was not a woman but was his younger brother who had been killed by the people of the place. Tamatea climbed the hill and played his lament there. Only a signpost remains to remind us of Tamatea-pokai-whenua, tribal ancestor, traveller, musician, man of the 14th century.

Aotea-tua-toru, Aotea the third. It takes its name from another carved house built in 1883 a few miles outside Dannevirke, Aotea-tua-rua, Aotea the second. Aotea the original meeting house was built many generations ago.

Aotea-tua-toru, Aotea III, was built in 1967 but the spirit of the two previous meeting houses is within it, carried in the form of the old carvings, cleaned and re-set.

PLATE 19   The longest place name near Porangahau in southern Hawke's Bay (*top*)
The Aotea-tua-toru Maori meeting house at Dannevirke (*lower*)

Reputedly known as the longest name in the world ...

TAUMATAWHAKATANGI HANGAKOAUAUOTAMATEA TURIPUKAKAPIKIMAUNGA HORONUKUPOKAIWHEN UAKITANATAHU

AA

← THE PLACE WHERE, TAMATEA, THE MAN WITH THE BIG KNEES, WHO SLID, CLIMBED, AND SWALLOWED MOUNTAINS, KNOWN AS LANDEATER, PLAYED HIS FLUTE, TO HIS LOVED ONE.
GUINNESS BOOK OF RECORDS... UNOFFICIAL VERSION

IN THE MUSEUM at Norsewood a distinctive strand in the pattern of Hawke's Bay is preserved in a display of household goods and farm equipment used by people from northern Europe set down in a forest in an island in the south Pacific.

The Museum building was built in 1888 and was the home of the Lutheran pastor. It was moved from an isolated site in 1965 and converted into a museum as a memorial to the pioneers of Norsewood.

The Government, in the 1870s, planned to open up New Zealand for settlement with an ambitious plan involving building a railway and making new towns along its length. This demanded the bringing to New Zeland of large numbers of settlers who could first clear the forests, then build the railway, then make farms and build towns and settle to rural and urban citizenship.

Such settlers were not too easy to find but Scandinavia proved a good place in which to seek them. Not only were the Scandinavians good lumber men but scarcity of fertile land had taught them to be frugal, and a harsh climate had made them hardy.

Even so, the cruel reality of what faced them in their new south sea home reduced many of them to hopeless tears. They were set down in a clearing in the heart of the Seventy Mile Bush and expected to make a start building the new New Zealand. Each family was sold 20 acres of land on deferred payment terms. To meet the debt they were required to work for the Government for several days a week at 5s. 0d. a day and the work was hard and heavy bush-clearing. On the other days they could work for themselves and begin the task of turning their 20 acres of forest section into a farm and a home.

They lay down at night in despair but they rose up every morning to work again and to plan. They cut back the forest and they established flourishing farms. They made their town. They laboured with a will because it was their own land on which they struggled; it was their own future they built. And they prospered.

The Norsewood Oak was planted in 1897 to mark twenty-five years of settlement, the turning of a nightmare into a realised dream.

PLATE 20   The Norsewood Pioneer Museum (*top*)
The oak tree at Norsewood (*lower*)

PORANGAHAU and Pourerere, coastal settlements between Cape Kidnappers and Cape Turnagain, are places steeped in history—European, Maori, pre-Maori history.

Ornaments found at Porangahau indicate that the district was occupied by Polynesians long before the Maori canoe migration of the 14th century.

Pourerere was the first sheep run to be taken up in Hawke's Bay and Captain Cook landed pigs and poultry and seed there in the 18th century and started an agricultural revolution.

To the coastal farmers of these areas, the sea was their life-line, the way out for their produce, the way in for their supplies. Behind them was a stretch of steep, difficult, un-roaded country.

Porangahau settlers in the 1860s built their own 15-ton ketch in the Porangahau stream and waited for a flood to come along to launch her on her way to the sea. For some years the little ship provided a link between the settlement and other places on the East Coast but she was wrecked in 1877—the usual end to small ships on this dangerous coast.

When a regular shipping line took on the coastal trade, the news that a ship was on its way was spread along the coast by a man on horseback. When the coaster appeared on the horizon she blew long blasts on her whistle and frantic activity broke out on shore. The whaleboat was run out of its shed into the water. Wool was loaded into bullock drays and the bulls were driven into the surf. The wool bales were manhandled from dray to long-boat, taken out through the breakers to the coaster and trans-shipped again for passage to Ahuriri and an overseas freighter.

When the ship sailed away she usually carried the result of a year's hard work and the hope of a year's pay. Attention was then turned to where the women and children were congregated, with the heap of unloaded stores on the beach waiting to be packed into the drays and taken to the homes . . . food, medicines, clothing, farm equipment, household goods . . . everything that might be needed during the months ahead until the next ship called.

And sometimes there was tragedy when heavy seas made the trans-shipping impossible and the coaster sounded a long farewell blast and sailed away again, the wool still waiting on the beach, the stores still in the hold.

PLATE 21   Farmlands at Porangahau (*top*)
Pastoral scene near Pourerere (*lower*)

At EVERY TURN at Maraekakaho there are reminders of the once-great Maraekakaho Station. In its day Maraekakaho was the colonial success story to cap them all.

Its founder was Donald McLean, a boy from a Hebridean island who became one of New Zealand's ablest administrators and most astute politicians. A successful and persuasive land-buyer for the Government, he acquired 30,000 acres for his own holding. He was as efficient at planning a farm as he was at planning political moves and when he died he left behind him a feudal estate self-contained and self-serviced, worked by specially imported people, many also from the Hebrides.

In one generation he made his son into a wealthy laird but in one generation more politics and land legislation had undone the work. In the compulsory breaking up of big estates the mighty Maraekakaho ceased to be the private domain of one man and was divided between about sixty small farmers, each unit becoming a prosperous farming proposition.

Maraekakaho Woolshed has a special place in the history of Hawke's Bay, one of the last surviving reminders of a period of social experiment rendered obsolete as it reached its peak. One of the largest shearing sheds in New Zealand, it was built in the 1880s, a stand shed with two boards of 14 stands each.

Fast work in the sheds was ensured by strong competition between man and man and between the teams from the two boards at opposite ends of the shed. At the end of each day tallies were read out and if bets were laid on the totals, the laird did not like to know about it.

The woolshed was the social centre for the district. The station in its heyday employed a permanent staff of nearly 100 and housed their families. There were also large numbers of seasonal workers, shearers and harvesters. Social affairs, dances, meetings, political rallies, were all held in the woolshed; marriages were made and political careers blighted . . . and vice versa.

PLATE 22 Maraekakaho village (*top*)
Maraekakaho woolshed (*lower*)

THERE are two crossings of the ranges from Hawke's Bay to the inland plateau of the North Island. The Taihape Road, the southern route, is today described on maps as a difficult road so it can easily be imagined what it was like last century when it was the only access route for settlers of the inland stations.

Getting wool out to market was for them a vast undertaking involving strings of pack mules carrying pockets of wool. At Kuripapango the wool was transferred to bullock wagons for its journey down to the coast and the mules turned for home laden with stores.

Kuripapango, surprisingly, became a fashionable holiday resort in the 1890s in spite of its difficult access. Ladies and children considered delicate were sent up for a few weeks of mountain air.

But the health resort image blossomed only for a short time. One night in 1901 the hotel was burned down, the guests were driven down through the hills to Napier in their night attire and Kuripapango again became just the meeting place for packmen and bullock drivers.

Now they too have passed into history and fast cars flash through Kuripapango on their way to Taihape. Few of their passengers give a thought to the full and varied life once lived there. Until recently, the Waipunga Falls were not visible from the Napier-Taupo road but in the making of a new deviation to by-pass a steep and difficult hill road, the Ministry of Works put in an extra piece of road to a look-out point and so opened up this lovely view to travellers.

There is a fund of stories about the Taupo Road and many of them are concerned with the soldiers stationed at the blockhouses through the ranges . . . the careless soldiers, killed while resting away from their arms; the hopeful soldiers planning to commercialise a hot spring; the aesthetic soldiers who built a little temple of the arts at their post with music, painting and literature. There are stories of grim endeavour to get the mail through by coach or by pony-mail, of parties of travellers escorted from one post to the next by armed troopers, of terrible experiences in flooded river, swamp or bush.

The building of this road was a nightmare task at the start when men laboured with shovels in the mud and clay and in spite of the use of great earth-moving machines one of the most difficult stretches was the last link in the sealed highway, the recently finished Runanga deviation.

The Ministry of Works received much merited praise for its environmental care in this piece of work. One of the contracts in the six-year undertaking was let for replanting, replacing, healing the damage done by the machines. Future generations will thank those who carried out public works and left the land undamaged.

PLATE 23   The old coaching inn at Kuripapango (*top*)
The Waipunga Falls (*lower*)

TUKITUKI STATION is typical of farming land in Hawke's Bay. With a balance of hills and flats it lends itself to sheep and cattle farming and to the production of grain and fodder crops.

This is a low rainfall area but ample water is available to stock and it is good healthy country.

The homestead is nearly a hundred years old and was reputed to be haunted on its original site. Seventy years ago it was moved eight miles by traction engine, crossing on its journey the wide Tukituki river. One theory had it that ghosts do not cross water.

The present owners, the Coop Family, have been prominent in equestrian sports for many years and a fine array of trophies bears witness to their successes. The house is mainly furnished in a style in keeping with its period and holds many interesting articles.

Sweeping lawns and colourful shrubberies accommodate a score of pea-fowl and splendid old trees and younger choice specimens play host to flights of ring-neck doves. Among the beautiful and colourful beds of flowers are many relics of pioneering days in New Zealand—trypots from a whaling station, ornate water troughs, millstones, lamp standards with fluted plaster columns, fine wooden gates and cast iron gates. Another lovely feature of the garden is an aga-panthus hedge—200 yards of sheer blue.

In a shady paddock, a fascinating collection of animals lives together in apparent harmony—a wild black pig, Red and Fallow deer, donkeys, tame sheep, goats and cattle and a mighty red and white bullock.

An old sheep, a ram with horns, knocks against a fence to draw attention to himself. Born with a genetic difference, he is the founder of a promising carpet-wool breed of sheep, the Tukidale. His progeny are being developed with scientific assistance and should eventually make an impact on the carpet trade.

The Tukituki valley, in which this farm is situated, is one of the most picturesque parts of Hawke's Bay and is much loved by artists and photographers.

PLATE 24 The Tukituki station homestead

TUNANUI RUN, 31,000 acres, was leased from its Maori owners in 1861 by the brothers, Capt. A. H. Russell and Capt. W. R. Russell and 2000 acres of it is still farmed by the Russell family.

They were a military family, soldiers and the sons of soldiers, educated at Sandhurst, serving with the Imperial forces in many parts of the world. The two brothers and their father, Col A. H. Russell, liked what they saw of New Zealand and its opportunities when their regiments served there so they left the Army and became pastoralists.

Because the habit of command and organisation was strong in them, they took a leading part in local and national affairs, in the formation of a new country, a new nation of people. And because they were good soldiers they made a good job of it and wove into the developing Hawke's Bay a sense of disciplined and dedicated service.

Colonel Russell was an active politican and administrator; William had a successful political career and became Leader of the Opposition and holder of various Cabinet portfolios; Hamilton's son was Major-General Sir Andrew Russell, G.O.C. of the N.Z. forces in the first war.

It was the General who planted the many fine trees on the Tunanui property and who applied military precision to the task of making a successful farming unit.

The Russell method was the Sandhurst mind at work. They were men trained in the standard military gambits for dealing with an enemy; trained to follow out the ground rules and to see that all subordinates did the same; to assess a given situation; to recognise one's own strengths and the weaknesses of the opposition; to act decisively, to take risks, to be always alert for the approach of a new threat.

It was an attitude that had painted large areas of the map of the world in red.

Applied to colonial farming and colonial politics, it worked very well.

PLATE 25   The Tunanui woolshed (foreground) and homestead at Sherenden

WESTSHORE, Napier's most popular bathing beach is a sweep of fine sand and calm water inside the harbour in marked contrast to the shingle banks and pounding surf of the beach alongside the business area of the town.

At times the beach is crowded but in this view two people have it to themselves in a world of sky and space and empty sea. There are not to many places left in the world where, within a couple of miles of the city centre, this kind of peace and solitude can be found.

Westshore's other public asset is its Wildlife Refuge in the Ahuriri Lagoon and this, also, is something of a surprise being close to the main north highway and partly within Napier city limits.

After the earthquake in 1931 raised the bed of the sea, an area of shallow ponds and tidal flats was left and these have developed into one of the finest wildlife refuges in the country. The ebb and flow of the tide through the lagoon offers an ever-changing habitat allowing some birds to breed, others to feed or to rest during migration. Twenty-four species of migratory wader are known at the Refuge, sometimes several hundred come in a group, stay for several months, travel from as far away as Siberia. Some extremely rare birds have been seen here for the first time in New Zealand.

The Hawke's Bay Wildlife Trust controls the Refuge by arrangement with the City Council. Not many cities the size of Napier are fortunate enough to have a wildlife reserve within their boundaries.

PLATE 26   A dramatic cloud formation over Westshore Beach

OCEAN BEACH is the first of the beaches to the south of Cape Kidnappers. This photograph looks north towards the Cape and the gannet sanctuary.

It is a wide and beautiful stretch of sand, one of the finest beaches in the country. Yet in the past it was the scene of hard work and considerable danger.

At the northern end of the beach is Rangaiika, site of a whaling station in the 1840s. Three boats and about twenty men of various nationalities as well as a number of Maoris worked out from the beach in the hunt for whales.

The catch was hauled up on to the beach to be stripped and boiled down; the sand was soaked with oil and the air filled with the stench from trying-down pots . . . and all to provide the ladies of other lands with corset bone and ribs for umbrellas and parasols, with candles and perfume.

Prior to the arrival of the whalers, this coast line was well populated and there is evidence of Maori occupation over many centuries and also of pre-Maori people. The sand dunes have yielded bone fragments from the extinct giant moa bird and the tuatara lizard as well as the sand-polished bones of men, ashes of cooking fires long cold, shells and bones that tell of mighty feasting with human bones as well as animal bones in the ashes, broken weapons telling of fights to the death.

Today, in summer, Ocean Beach is a scene of tents and beach umbrellas and car awnings with a busy surf club keeping guard on the swimmers. Once, long ago, people came there in hordes in search of kai moana, food from the sea. Now they come with winter-pale skins to swim and lie in the sun and turn themselves into copies of the bare brown bodies of earlier centuries.

PLATE 27   Ocean Beach looking north towards Cape Kidnappers

THIS VIEW of Waimarama is typical of many places on the coast of Hawke's Bay . . . looking from the crest of a hill to a line of surf, a sandy beach and the blue ocean.

Waimarama is one of the most popular beaches of Hawke's Bay. Access to it is good and in the summer months it is much frequented by surfers and swimmers. A township of holiday cottages comes to life and surf-patrols are kept on the alert.

Waimarama is a word that rolls softly and pleasantly from the tongue. Romantics, especially young ones on a warm summer evening when the moon is full and the sea is calm, like to translate it as 'moonlit water'.

When Captain Cook sailed along the coast of Hawke's Bay he noted that the coastal country behind these beaches was not the usual forest-clad and secretive place but more like rolling English downs above sandy shores. He recorded that it was well populated and he saw smoke rising from many Maori villages. The Maoris who came out in their canoes and boarded his ship were friendly and dignified, They had tattooed faces, wore their hair done up in top-knots pierced with feathers and wore greenstone neck ornaments, "pellucid, like an emerald" Others would not come aboard. They followed the *Endeavour* in 20-man canoes shouting insults and waving their weapons and challenging the larger vessel to stand and fight.

Bare Island, off Waimarama, was then Motuakoura, crayfish island, a place of good fishing and a safe refuge in time of attack. The French explorer, D'Urville, in 1827, described it as an escarped rock, naked and impregnable. He called it L'Ile Sterile, Bare Island.

Today the sea comes up in long rollers on to the sandy beaches and there is no sign that either sailing vessel or canoe ever cut its waters. Holidaymakers swim and sunbathe, fishermen have the ocean to themselves and Cook, D'Urville and the long-dead rangatiras are alike forgotten.

PLATE 28   Waimarama Beach (*top*)
Kairakau Beach (*lower*)

THE MOST BEAUTIFUL beaches of Hawke's Bay are often the most inaccessible, a fact about which people who farm in those areas are sometimes very glad. Waipatiki, pictured here, and its neighbour in the next valley, Aropaoanui, lie on the open coast to the north of Ahuriri Harbour. The access to both is by miles of steep, winding, narrow road but when the highway was the sea-lane, these were important ports of call for canoes. The name Waipatiki means flounder fishing ground and the remains of a Maori village can be seen on the hill above the beach.

The first wave of European settlers came into Waipatiki in 1912 and the next wave came after World War I—veterans of Gallipoli looking for the good life on their own farms promised by a grateful government. Many of them were South Canterbury men who travelled the country on a free pass looking for the cheapest land in New Zealand, knowing that this meant the most difficult land in New Zealand, or the most inaccessible. They settled for northern Hawke's Bay and land near a beautiful beach reached by a tortuous Maori track.

More than a hundred years ago the track to northern Hawke's Bay and Wairoa followed the beaches and the cliff tops of the coast and then a few weary but determined travellers, the missionaries, the pack-men, the mail-man with his bags strapped to his saddle, were seen in the settlements.

Aropaoanui was settled in 1862 by John McKinnon, a seaman from the Outer Hebrides who, after an adventurous life all over the oceans of the world, sailed the New Zeland coast and tried his hand at many things including whaling before he leased his coastal run, with its cliff-tops from which the whalers had kept their look out for the sightings, and stocked it with sheep. He soon found that farming, too, had its hazards and he was down to his last cent with ruin staring him in the face when the sea came to his rescue. The master of a ship in the Bay died suddenly and McKinnon took the command, sailed her home to England and returned with enough money to save his run and go on to prosper.

PLATE 29   Waipatiki Beach

MAHIA PENINSULA curves round the northern part of Hawke's Bay. Its splendid sandy beaches are rarely crowded becauses of its distance from the centres of population.

Mahia is an area steeped in history, the heartland of Hawke's Bay Maoris. On some of its inaccessible cliff-tops, visible only to the airborne sightseer, can be seen the earthworks of fortified villages dating back to the 12th century and before.

Whatonga, captain of the Kurahaupo canoe, settled at Mahia after bringing his canoe over the ocean from Eastern Polynesia. He chose Mahia because it offered him two full foodbaskets to serve his needs—the ocean and the forest.

In the 14th century, Kahungunu, the ancestor from whom Hawke's Bay Maoris take their tribal name, also lived at Mahia. Kahungunu could be the idol of today as he was of the people of his own day for he had many of the qualities much admired in the top people of entertainment and politics. He was tall and handsome, he wore his hair long and done up in a fashionable top-knot, he was amiable and fun-loving. He was a good practical man and he was able to teach others to lay out villages in proper order, to plan irrigation and drainage, to organise the times for hunting and fishing. He was a Viking of the Pacific who understood the sea and its moods and seasons, knew how to build canoes and navigate long distances. He encouraged carving and weaving and oratory, the social arts. He excelled in everything he did and he was much given to marrying, a firm believer in making love rather than war. As a result, he made family ties and tribal links along the whole of the East Coast and he achieved more unity in his way than his more warlike contemporaries did in theirs.

In the early years of the 19th century Mahia was the place in Hawke's Bay where it was all happening. Many Maoris, driven from their homes on the plains by tribes from the north armed with muskets, sought refuge at Mahia. In the 1820s a European flax-trader was employing them to scrape flax and prepared it for trading ships buying for the Australian ropeworks to supply the needs of sailing ships.

In the 1830s whalers brought greed and disease to Mahia. In the 1840s came the missionaries with word of a better way of life. In the 1850s came the settlers and they settled, not at Mahia, but near the harbour at Ahuriri. And the Maori people returned to the plains and moved finally into the world of European commerce.

PLATE 30   The Mahia Peninsula from Opoutama Beach (*top*)
Looking north along the West coast of the Mahia Peninsula (*lower*)

AUTUMN on the Ruataniwha Plains, the rich alluvial flats built out of the bounty of the Tukituki river.

Waipukurau town stands on the south bank of the river and even in pre-European days it was an important place for it was the ford at which the Maori trail crossed the river.

A large block of land on Ruataniwha was taken up in the 1850s by H. R. Russell who formed an ambition to lay out a model township. The start of Waipukurau in 1867 was this plan put into practice. Russell built cottages and leased sections of land and he brought tradesmen and artisans from England to be his model townsmen. He imposed firm restrictions on entry into his community so that there would be but one man in each trade and so all would live in peace and harmony.

Russell was a man of the 19th century who saw himself in the role of a benevolent squire of the 18th century. For a few years he sustained the role but the Liberal government of the 1890s thought otherwise. Compulsory acquisition of land was introduced and large, one-man estates were reduced into many smaller holdings.

Waipukurau ceased to be the dream town of one man and became a busy open township serving a prosperous farming community and milling, quarrying and engineering industries.

The view from Pukeora Hill is made pleasant by beautiful trees along the course of the river. Many of them were planted long ago in the heyday of H. R. Russell and have survived the passing of the colonial dream and lived to grace the modern reality.

PLATE 31   Pukeora hill, looking towards Waipukurau

THE LEADING TOWN of southern Hawke's Bay, Dannevirke lies in the upper valley of the Manawatu river to the east of the Ruahine range.

The railway and the main north-south highway pass through Dannevirke and long ago, when the district lay deep within the Seventy Mile Bush, the Maori track linking the Manawatu with Hawke's Bay passed through.

Dannevirke is a railway town. The great Public Works Plan of a hundred years ago launched New Zealand into the world of modern transport and communication and its foundation was a plan to import immigrants from Europe in large numbers, put them to work clearing a track for the railway—felling forest, cutting sleepers, laying track—and then make land for settlement available for them along the path of the railway.

The plan failed in many parts of New Zealand but it was successful in Hawke's Bay.

The Maori owners, with tears, parted with the bush and they bitterly regretted it when they saw what was to happen. In October, 1872, the first families moved into the bush and started work in tears of hopeless despair. Twenty-one families of Danes were taken through thick forest and rocky gorge, across deep rivers, to be deposited in a clearing in the bush—the start of Dannevirke. No one seems to have recalled that Denmark is not forest country and that they were unused to lumbering.

The name Dannevirke had historic associations for the new settlers. The Dannevirke was a great defensive wall built across the southern neck of the Jutland peninsula in the 8th century to fend off Saxon invasion. It was strengthened in the 12th century by an additional brick rampart. It must have seemed fitting to the new settlers to use the name of their ancient fortification in their task of driving back and holding back the forest.

The immigrants proved to be tough and determined to survive. They cut back the forest and made pasture land, they built an industry on the timber and they made a town which is today the centre of a prosperous sheep and dairy district with many associated industries.

But most of all, the Danes at Dannevirke—and the Swedes and Norwegians of the adjoining settlements—brought an infusion of North European steadiness to their new country as well as great love and loyalty.

PLATE 32 High Street, Dannevirke (*top*)
Dannevirke gardens (*lower*)

THE NAME WAIROA—the long river—goes back to the 14th century and the coming to the east coast of Takitimu canoe, the canoe in which the ancestors of Hawke's Bay Maoris migrated from their island homeland.

Takitimu rode over the river bar and up the Wairoa River to the spot where Takitimu meeting house now stands.

The coming of the canoe was no small matter for this was a craft carrying a specially chosen crew of high-born chiefs rich in knowledge and wisdom and the ancient lore of their race. Wherever the canoe put to shore these men, in special rituals which involved the lighting of ceremonial fires, implanted into the land, the mauri, the life-giving spirit of their people, something of more value in a migration than all the seeds and weapons and artifacts carried by the canoes.

And the life-force, once implanted, may sleep but it never leaves the place.

Wairoa stands mid-way between Napier and Gisborne and across the lines of communication between Mahia Peninsula, Lake Waikaremoana, Morere Hot Springs and the coastal settlements. Today it enjoys good access by road and is a tourist junction but it still retains something of the independent, self-reliant spirit forced upon it by years of isolation when access by sea was sometimes made impossible by the blocking of the river bar and access by land was possible only to the most determined traveller who could hack a way through a wilderness of scrub and man-high fern.

Wairoa's first Europeans were flax-traders, then came the whalers and an influx of nameless men, runaway seamen, time-expired convicts, men who found the isolation of the district no hardship but rather an advantage.

Formal settlement began in 1865 and a handful of farmers, tradesmen and shopkeepers lived comfortably with a river full of fish, all kinds of sea-goods, a lagoon abundant with swamp birds and a bush area full of pigeon and other birds.

Settlement was slow, impeded by Maori reluctance to sell land and by war and rebellion swirling around the district but today Wairoa is a pleasant and comfortable town supported by its rural area and its primary production.

PLATE 33 Wairoa from the river bank (*top*)
The town bridge and lighthouse at Wairoa (*lower*)

HAVELOCK NORTH has long since graduated from the status of a village as far as size is concerned but it is hanging on to the description with determination as far as atmosphere is concerned.

It has been described as the town that missed the train but retained its soul.

A hundred years ago it was doing very well in the no-holds-barred competition for importance as a provincial centre. It stood a fair chance of having the railway come through and everyone knew that where the railway went trade and development would follow.

Hastings—three miles away across the plains—won the railway and, as predicted, started its growth into a flourishing city. Havelock finally came to wear its village identity as a decoration and to foster a set of values not solely commercial.

Much of its charm it owes to the tree-planting enthusiasm of its earliest settlers, notably Thomas Tanner. The pin-oak beside St. Luke's church, one of Tanner's plantings, figures in the national record of historic trees.

The private schools of Havelock North have become nationally famous. Theatre, music and art have always flourished at an amateur but extremely high level. There have always been writers in Havelock North as well as potters and sculptors and painters. And there have usually been groups of exponents of avant garde religious and health beliefs.

A town laid out in carefully haphazard fashion, Havelock North is a place of tree-lined streets, grass verges rather than pavements and many fine houses and beautiful gardens tucked into the folds of its sunny hillside. Waipawa is the centre of one of New Zealand's most prosperous farming districts. It produces fat lambs and cattle and grows large areas of barley, wheat, ryegrass and clover. Most of the wheat grown in Hawke's Bay is grown in the Waipawa district and many farmers get a crop of grass seed late in the year from paddocks grazed by their ewes and lambs early in the year.

There was a time in the early years of settlement when people living at Napier referred to a trip to Waipawa—forty miles—as a journey into the interior, only to be undertaken by the strong and venturesome. Then, wool and grain were shipped downriver in canoes and whaleboats to their markets and supplies were brought up to the township in the same way.

PLATE 34   The township of Havelock North (*top*)
Looking over Waipawa (*lower*)

LEGISLATION to protect wildlife in New Zealand goes right back to the early years of settlement. Acclimatisation of selected birds and fish from Europe went hand in hand with measures for the protection of indigenous species. Government could pass legislation concerning these matters but it had little finance to spare and the work cost some settlers a geat deal in time and money.

The Tukituki Wildlife Refuge is an old-established refuge, being gazetted more than fifty years ago. It stretches five miles up river from the Waimarama Bridge over the Tukituki River and is administered by the Department of Internal Affairs Wildlife Division and supervised by the local Acclimatisation Society.

The Refuge lies between river and road and is interlaced with many quiet backwaters and flood channels which provide a haven for duck, pied stilt, game pheasant, dotterel and various species of shag.

The restriction on the area relates only to wildlife and the area is a favourite trout fishing spot. The Tukituki is usually considered a Rainbow trout river but Brown trout weighing up to eighteen pounds have been caught in it. Fish reaching this size are thought to have lived in the lower reaches of the river where sea food is abundant.

PLATE 35   A view of the Tukituki Wildlife Reserve from Esthorpe Road

LAKE TUTIRA is a Wildlife Refuge lying between Napier and Wairoa. Its environs are a public domain and are controlled by a domain board.

The block of poor land in which it is situated took its name from the lake and became Tutira Station, subject of a well-known book. It broke the heart of a number of settlers who tried to tame it and wrest a living from a wilderness of bracken and fern and it finally yielded its riches to the man who loved it and wooed it, studied its moods and wrote in its praise, W. H. Guthrie-Smith.

Long before the European came to Tutira it was known as a plentiful food supply and its shores were dotted with Maori settlements. It is a place rich in history and stories of sacred places for secret ritual, water monsters, tribal feuds, eel weirs and eel houses, of canoes paddling silently over the lake in the night, mostly on matters of vengeance but sometimes on matters of love.

The past haunts the present at Lake Tutira. People still talk of the floating island appearing in different parts of the lake although assured there is no such island. They marvel about what is known to Maoris as the mahia Tutira, to Europeans as the Tutira telephone, a sound-carrying property of the lake surface by which voices can be heard over a mile of water.

Sadly, Tutira today is a lake with a problem. Due to plankton growth, there is only a very narrow band of oxygen during the summer months and fish are restricted to this band.

However, the local Acclimatisation Society restocks the lake annually with rainbow trout fingerlings and the Department of Agriculture is working on a scheme to circulate oxygen in the lake and restore it to full life.

Guthrie-Smith read in the changes he recorded over Tutira a warning that both land and water would die if man did not learn to co-operate with nature.

Lovers of this beautiful lake hope that the lesson has been learned here in time and that Tutira will remain for future generations a lake of living water.

PLATE 36 Lake Tutira

THERE ARE thirty gannetries round the coast of New Zealand but that at Cape Kidnappers is the only one not on an island. During the breeding season gannets usually settle on an island well away from the possibility of disturbance but in Hawke's Bay they choose the seaward sloping peninsula of Cape Kidnappers at the southern tip of the Bay.

The gannets make a striking picture—white with golden crowns and black-tipped flight feathers. With curved beaks and eyes outlined in black, they sit exactly two feet apart, as far as they can conveniently peck from a sitting position. Anyone—human or bird—who comes within two feet can expect to be pecked.

The gannets of Cape Kidnappers do not seem to miss the privacy so sought by the birds of an island gannetry. Every day, carefully timing the tide, people walk or drive in beach buggies along the edge of the surf under the high cliffs split by previous earthquake movement; above them, on the cliff top, others ride ponies or drive in a safari wagon. And they're all heading for the same place . . . out to the Cape to see the gannets. Visitors watch the birds in their ritual displays and see them making dramatic high dives from incredible heights in search of fish; they see them assiduously guarding their eggs in the crowded colony.

It is a heartening fact that though the birds at Cape Kidnappers have trusted humanity enough to make their colony in the vicinity of two cities and a string of popular holiday beaches, they have not been taken advantage of. Local authorities and the public co-operate all the way in a determination to protect the bird sanctuary and its colony.

PLATE 37   Nesting gannets on flat rocks at Black Reef, near Cape Kidnappers

THE CATHEDRAL OF ST JOHN THE EVANGELIST, in Napier, is the parish church of Napier city and the cathedral of Waiapu diocese. The first St. John's was built in 1862 and in 1888 was replaced by an impressive brick cathedral. This was completely destroyed in the 1931 earthquake and for more than twenty-five years a timber church was in use until the present cathedral was completed in 1965. In it, modern materials and technology are used in a traditional plan. It contains many gift items of historic interest and has a particularly fine organ.

ST. MARY'S CHURCH, Greenmeadows, is the successor to a small wooden building at nearby Meeanee, the mother church of all the Catholic churches of Hawke's Bay. A sole relic of the old church, its bell, is mounted high on the wall of the new. This sweeping design was influenced by the traditional open-arm style of a Maori meeting-house. The spiral plan with entrance courtyard encircled as though by welcoming arms provides for fan-shaped seating which integrates the congregation with the altar and its service.

This modern church at Woodville is dedicated to THE HOLY TRINITY and it displays traditional early colonial gothic influence in a modern design. The original church was built in 1886 and its first vicar was the pioneer Hawke's Bay missionary William Colenso. Woodville is the first town in Hawke's Bay through which the traveller from the south passes when he emerges from the Manawatu Gorge.

ST. JOSEPH'S church in Clive was built in 1889 and is serviced by the Hastings Catholic parish. It is a fine example of the typical colonial gothic wooden church and the height it is built above the ground explains why Clive did not develop as hoped. At the time the church was built, Clive was a promising town with a meat works, two breweries, a flour mill, market gardens, a dairy factory and a small trading steamer, the *Bella*, working up and down the river. Disastrous flooding in the 1890s brought an end to all this promise.

St. Joseph's was seriously damaged by fire in 1974 and the action of the Anglican and Presbyterian parishes in sharing their church facilities until St. Joseph's was repaired kindled a great warmth of Christian fellowship in Clive.

PLATE 38   St John's Cathedral, Napier (*left*)
St Mary's Church, Greenmeadows (*right*)
The Holy Trinity Church, Woodville (*lower left*)
St Joseph's Church, Clive (*lower right*)

SOME of New Zealand's best-known schools are in Hawke's Bay. In the past they helped to make the provincial character and today they can still be seen as formative influences.

Te Aute College was founded in 1854, a missionary school. In the 1890s a remarkable group of its pupils emerged as the Young Maori Party; they were lawyers and doctors who became politicians and writers and who led their people towards a new way of life in which they moved freely in two cultures, utilising the best features of both.

The name Te Aute commemorates the paper mulberry tree, the great provider of clothing and fabric in an earlier Polynesian homeland. It failed to acclimatise in New Zealand and a substitute was found in the native flax which proved even more useful and adaptable.

But the name remains—Te Aute—symbol of the life-preserving gifts of earlier times, of the need to look for a new way when the old ways fail, of the things of the present which, enriched with knowledge and awareness, can replace the lost ways of the past.

Te Aute, where the gifts from the past are used to illuminate and replenish the good things of the present and offer hope for the future.

Woodford House was founded in 1894 by a teacher from England who observed that Hawke's Bay was a large rural area, the daughters of which could only be properly educated in a centrally situated boarding school. The farmers who were fathers of such daughters fully agreed and helped Miss Hodge to build her school and transform 16 acres of barren Havelock North hillside into the beautiful parkland it is today.

Woodford House has become part of the fabric of rural Hawke's Bay but it also has read the signs of the times and adapted to them. In a realisation that Hawke's Bay is not made up of two types of people—rural and urban—but is a working partnership of the two, a new aim has developed. It is another version of the Te Aute motivating force, to move freely between two ways and select what is best from each.

PLATE 39   Te Aute College (*top*)
Woodford House (*lower*)

THEY say that in Hawke's Bay you can enjoy yourself in, on, under or near water and certainly there is a wide variety of water recreation available.

The yachts in the photograph are sailing at Scapa Flow in the inner harbour at Ahuriri. Trawlers lie in to the wharf. The basin has been dredged and enlarged to provide mooring spaces for bigger boats but many families tow down their sailer-trailer to the harbour and then take it home again to garage.

Hawke's Bay children can learn to sail from the age of eight and many of them make a start in a one-man, seven-foot P-class boat. From there they can rise up through the various classes of boat right up to the sleek keelers designed for ocean racing.

Power boats use the harbour as well as the river and water skiing is popular on both.

Big-game fishing takes the larger boats out to sea for up to twenty miles in search of tuna and shark, snapper and grouper, and, hopefully, marlin. This is a sport for experienced hands as there is no shelter in the Bay and when the wind rises quickly the boats must run for port as fast as they can.

Swimming is probably the most popular of the water sports. Napier has sea-water baths as well as its Olympic Pool and Hastings has an excellent Aquatic Centre. Most schools have swimming pools and some of these are available to the public. Hawke's Bay has numerous swimming clubs and has produced some national swimming champions. Four life-saving clubs perform a service to the public by patrolling the four main beaches.

The Hawke's Bay Surf Association, helped by local service clubs, has introduced to unpatrolled beaches neoprene tubes made of foam rubber. These, with rope attached, can be clipped to the body of a person in difficulties who can then be hauled in by even an inexperienced life-saver.

Water safety measures are ensuring that Hawke's Bay remains an ideal place for water sports.

PLATE 40 Power boating on the river at Clive (*top*)
Yachting at Scapa Flow in the inner harbour at Ahuriri, Napier (*lower*)

THIS PICTURE of painters at work on Marine Parade, Napier, shows artists and would-be artists in light-hearted mood, painting instant masterpieces which will be auctioned on the spot for charity at prices reflecting more on the generosity of the buyers than the talent of the artists. A pavement artists contest is also held and gives an indication of remarkable talent for drawing among visiting holidaymakers and local children alike.

In Napier the Hawke's Bay Art Galley and Museum is the centre for the visual arts, music, history, craftwork. The Society has 130 painters working and exhibiting—and selling—and several hundred student members showing their work in their own exhibition and working towards admission as artist members. A professional tutor takes day-time classes, many members of which are housewives unable to attend regular evening classes.

The potters' group has its own studio and workshop and although some of its members are well-established potters known throughout the country they still teach the art to new members. Other groups are working on textile work and design, on carving, on spinning and weaving. Napier's Marineland is billed as the sea circus of the South Pacific and its performers are dolphins, fur seals and leopard seals.

The seals are seasoned troupers with versatile comedy acts and a thirst for applause but the favourites with the public are undoubtedly the dolphins with their graceful precision act.

Common dolphins are easily caught in Hawke's Bay and appear to enjoy their relationship with humanity. Training them to perform is not difficult being based on their natural behaviour and fondness for play. Trainers and spectators alike respond warmly to the strange natural affinity between man and dolphin, a gentle, affectionate partnership.

Marineland staff have no fear of dolphins and are adamant that a dolphin would never attack a human. Divers at work laying a pipe on the sea-bed not far from Marineland can attest to this. Their work was continually interrupted by dolphins enthusiastically saving them when they did not want to be saved and pushing them up to the surface every time they tried to stay down.

Marineland is not a zoo and it is more than a circus. Visitors walk away puzzled by the warmth of their feelings for the gentle dolphins.

PLATE 41   A holiday painting competition in progress on the Marine Parade, Napier (*top*)
A performing dolphin at Napier's Marineland (*lower*)

FANTASYLAND is a continuing project by Hastings citizens for the enjoyment of children and parents alike. Service Clubs, professional groups, private citizens and commercial interests, as well as Hastings City have financed play projects. These include the Fantasyland Castle, complete with turrets, battlements and moat, a play mountain with 86 feet of tunnels through tons of rock and concrete, a tree house complete with fireman's pole for a quick exit.

Noddyland is a miniature village for the smaller children and the next project is the development of Tomorrowland, a playground for space-age children. Enthusiasts for adventure playgrounds are hard at work planning suitably imaginative projects for this area.

The Hastings Parks Department is working on the belief that beauty of surroundings makes any play project better and has planted out colourful beds of flowers. Fantasyland is set in beautiful parkland and parents resting under the trees while their children play—free of charge—out in the sun, are inclined to agree that the natural pleasures take a lot of beating.

PLATE 42   Fantasyland at Hastings

HASTINGS and its surrounding district can fairly claim to be one of the main equestrian centres of New Zealand.

The headquarters of the New Zealand Horse Society is in Hastings and has been since its inception in 1950.

Show-jumping is a popular sport in Hawke's Bay perhaps because many riders are also farmers who use their horses as hacks on the farm and in the showring during the summer. Because they have ridden since childhood they are often bold and forceful horsemen—and women—who ride and jump with confidence.

Pony Clubs to teach children to ride and care for their horses started in 1945. The first, Heretaunga Pony Club, was a Hawke's Bay club and the movement has now spread throughout New Zealand and is providing a continuous stream of good competition riders.

Hunting got away to an early start in Hawke's Bay. The founding date of the Hawke's Bay Hunt is in doubt but it was operative in 1890 and so was the Dannevirke Hunt. The Mahia Hunt is also active. Fields of up to a hundred riders in a hunt are common.

The Hawke's Bay Hunt now has 106 acres of farmland supporting a complex of kennels, stables and other buildings and its pack of hounds is considered to be one of the best in the country. The East Coast area in general is a prime breeding ground for good hunters.

The Hawke's Bay Polo Club was formed in the early 1900s and many of its players have represented New Zealand.

The breeding of thoroughbreds and horse-racing play a major part in the sporting life of Hawke's Bay. Many famous racehorses have been bred at the well-known studs of the province, many of which are situated in the limestone country round Hastings. Hastings has a Metropolitan Jockey Club which races on fourteen days in the year. Very good stakes and excellent appointments attract good horses and the racing public who come from far and near on every race day are always certain of a good day's sport.

PLATE 43   A race meeting at Hastings

THE RUAHINE RANGE is part of the massive mountainous backbone of the North Island and the Wakarara Range is a much smaller but still very rugged range on its north-eastern side.

The area between these ranges was once a vast forest out of which over fifty million feet of native timber was cut, hauled out first by bullock and horse, later by steam traction engine. In recent years an effort has been made to regenerate the desolated land by scattering pineseeds from the air.

After the murder of the bush on so large a scale it is surprising to know that there are people who think that the huia bird, believed to be extinct, may still exist in the Wakarara area.

The huia had a certain mystique of its own. In pre-European times its white-tipped feathers were much prized, a symbol of rank reserved for the use of chiefs. Most portraits and drawings of 19th century Maoris of rank show the two huia feathers at the back of the head. The last recorded sighting was early this century and that in the Wakarara district but a few people since believe they have heard the call from which the bird got its name—huia.

The Ruahines rise to over 5000 feet and are visually very solid, forming an effective barrier between Hawke's Bay and the Inland plateau of the North Island. A few hardy settlers once took land in the Ruahines and unexpected beds of flowers, traces of domestic gardens with trees and shrubs, mark a place where once someone tried to make a home.

This is an accessible range of mountains with a number of roads leading up into the foothills, with mountain huts and marked tracks to attract trampers and shooters, but not a place to be taken casually. People familiar with that other world of alpine plants and rocks and tarns all tell tales of sudden blizzards and times when survival depended on wind-proof coats and warm woollen clothing while, down below, on the farmlands, the sun was still shining.

The Ruahines is one of the areas of New Zealand used by organised safaris catering for overseas hunting parties.

PLATE 44   Beef cattle eating winter feed with the snow capped peaks of the Ruahine Range in the distance (*top*)
Wakarara Range (*lower*)

FISHERMEN speak of the Manga-o-nuku river as a truly fine trout stream. It has a good supply of bottom feed providing first-class hatches of fly and a good rise in the evenings. Fish are not much seen during the day but with the approach of dusk they rise abundantly and provide excellent sport for the patient angler. Brown trout weighing up to 4 lbs are regularly taken from this river which has plentiful reaches of quiet water.

Argyll East is a farming community on the side of the Raukawa Range about six miles from the north-south highway. It is one of the settlements brought into being by legislation for closer settlement and it was balloted for in 1903. One block of 33,000 acres was divided into sixty-two farms in two settlements—Argyll East and Argyll West, one on each side of the Manga-o-nuku river.

At the start of the settlements Tikokino with its sawmills was the nearest marketing area and Argyll farmers derived some income from the sale of farm produce to sawmillers. Because so many heavy horses worked in the bush hauling out timber to the sawmills, Argyll became an oat-growing area. This was never a very successful form of farming. Farmers soon found that oat-growing was a vicious circle; to work horses hard you have to feed them oats and to cut oats into chaff you have to work horses hard . . . and feed them oats. . . .

The last thirty years is a happier story with scrub land being transformed into highly-prized farmland. The use of clover and the practice of top-dressing have made it into first-class country for cropping and for fat-lamb raising for the meat export trade.

And, whether farmers are successful or not, whether horses or tractors do the work, whether the district grows oats or fat lambs, the fish still lie in the quiet reaches and rise in the evenings and the fishermen still take time off to catch them.

PLATE 45   The Manga-o-nuku River at Argyll East

AUTUMN gilds the poplars at Whanawhana on the upper reaches of the Ngaruroro river.

In this photograph, the Ngaruroro meanders over a shingly bed nearly a mile wide but in time of flood it can cover the bed from bank to bank, a mighty and irresistible torrent of water. A few miles upriver the water is confined to narrow gorges strewn with boulders, the debris of previous floods, a fearful place when the water runs high but a fisherman's dream at the right times.

The river rises in the remote centre of the North Island between the Kaimanawa and Kaweka ranges in open country of pumice terraces and rolling hills covered in golden-red tussock, an unforgettable sight when lit by early-morning or late-afternoon sunlight. From here the river flows alternately south-east in great gorges cutting directly across the grain of the mountain folds and south-west in deep valleys between them. Many of the original place-names of Hawke's Bay are descriptive of natural features and Whana-whana, meaning to twist and turn, is a fair description of the river's course before it emerges on to the plains.

The Ngaruroro provides a water supply better than anything man could have devised. At some time of catastrophe in the past great floods laid down alternating beds of clean shingle and heavy clay over much of the area of the Heretaunga Plains. The water of the river filters down through these aquifers to come up clean and clear from artesian bores wherever it is needed to supply the cities and the industries. Up to half the summer flow of the river may run underground and what is not drawn off emerges in fresh-water springs off the coast.

It is a peaceful and pastoral scene in the photograph but without this river and its bounty both cities and plains would die.

PLATE 46   Whanawhana and the Ngaruroro River

AUTUMN AT DARTMOOR, a picture taken from the Dartmoor Bridge which crosses the Mangaone River, the main tributary of the Tutaekuri River, just before the confluence of the two.

The boulder-strewn Mangaone became a river highway in 1862 when the obstructions in its course were cleared away and the waterway left open with nothing to impede floating timber. This meant that a large area of bush at Pohue could be worked and totara posts for fencing could be cut and split and rafted downriver to buyers. Prior to the clearing of the Mangaone all this timber had been locked away for want of a means of getting it out.

After the opening of the waterway, about three rafts of timber a year were taken downriver, moving very slowly, taking weeks on the passage. Each raft contained about 10,000 posts and was managed by twelve men who delivered as ordered at places along the river. At the seaward end of the Tutaekuri a floating boom above Meeanee Bridge caught the remaining posts. Using punt poles and boat hooks the men moved the huge raft only a mile a day. They had to be strong and hardy men for the work although one of them, Corky Charley, a well-known character, had only one leg.

If a flood came during the river transit nothing could save the raft and the Meeanee boom was powerless to halt the rush. The posts would be washed downriver and out to sea and up on beaches all along the coast. Many lucky settlers got a free supply of fencing and beachcombers were busy for weeks after the flood.

The Tutaekuri River, into which the Mangaone flows, now goes out to sea, by man's decision, near Clive, but it was once the river of Napier, flowing along the boundary of the town and out to sea in the harbour. For about ten years at the start of the century the Tutaekuri was the tool of a reclamation syndicate in reclaiming a large area of land from swampy lagoon and providing space out on to which Napier was built.

PLATE 47   The Mangaone River at Dartmoor

THE MOHAKA RIVER rises in a heavily bush-covered and inaccessible area not far to the south-east of Lake Taupo. It flows through gorges deeply cut into hard rock as it passes the northern end of the Kaweka Range. This picture shows the Mohaka lower down its course where it flows through an area of much younger mudstones and siltstones.

This is a river with an exceptionally steep gradient and hydro-electric engineers have looked with longing at its narrow, easily-dammed gorges but have realised that the numerous earthquake faults in this area would render large dams unsafe.

The settlement known as Mohaka was built on the river flats close to the sea. It was an isolated settlement served only from the sea and in the Maori uprisings of the 1860s only courageous people would live there. A blockhouse was built near the river mouth as a place of refuge in time of attack but in spite of this sixty people, many of them Maori, were killed there in a raid in 1869.

Further inland, back up the river where it cuts through the gorges, there was once a period of great activity and excitement.

A century ago, early settlers, hungry for their share of the gold being taken so freely from other parts of the North Island, began prospecting in Hawke's Bay and they found traces of gold—they 'saw the colour'—near the deeply-cut gorges and swift-flowing waters of the Mohaka.

The speculators invested, the miners drilled and blasted and tunnelled and the prospectors waded up the icy tributaries with axe and pan. And every ship into Napier brought miners from Australia and all parts of New Zealand ready to join in the rush on the Mohaka.

But it was all to no avail. Even though the riches of the Mohaka were said to include silver and platinum and copper as well as gold, nothing came of all the hopeful seeking. Finally, the packhorses plodded back into town, the investors counted their losses and the prospectors walked on over the ranges looking for a better prospect, sure that the next find would be the real find.

Defying the hopes of the gold-seekers as it would later those of the electricity-seekers, the Mohaka flowed on between the high walls of its gorges down to the wide river flats and the sea; its secrets, if it has any, inviolate.

PLATE 48   The Mohaka River

I N THIS BEAUTIFUL SCENE the setting sun casts a golden glow on gum trees and poplars near Frasertown in northern Hawke's Bay.

Many of the early settlers of Hawke's Bay were dedicated tree-planters. Sometimes they planted for practical reasons but often their reasons were purely sentimental. These were the trees of home and they sought to bring something of their old life into their new land.

The willow was much favoured by settlers because it was quick-growing and easily propagated and could be cut down to provide emergency stock food during drought. It is the harbinger of spring, bare of leaves for only a few short weeks and so now almost an evergreen, a tree which has adapted magnificently to a changed environment.

The poplar also grew quickly and easily. Fresh-cut poplar poles were often used for fence posts to eventually grow into a row of shelter trees and long straight rows of poplars along the edge of the paddocks soon made an alien landscape into something familiar and reassuring. In time of flood they trapped the silt from the floodwaters sweeping over the land and compensated for the damage done with a generous coating of silt-soil.

Eucalypts, mainly Tasmanian blue-gum, were brought across the Tasman at an early date. They were chiefly in demand as a timber tree but in a kinder climate than that of their native home they grew to a new height and beauty and became valued for their delicate shape and foliage. In this scene, the stark beauty of trunk and branch peeled off their bark is seen at its best.

Introduced trees, once strangers on land stripped of its natural growth ...now a real and beautiful part of the New Zealand landscape.

To bring the good things of the past to the making of the future. That's what it's all about.

PLATE 49   Gums and poplars near Frasertown in northern Hawke's Bay

S TILL the rivers bring down shingle from the mountains
and the restless tide still piles it on the beach.

The moon looked just the same when the first canoes
rode the waves and grounded on the shingle in the harbour
under the shelter of the bluff, when the crews put their feet
on the shore and claimed it and offered sacrifice and implanted their life force in the land and knew this for a good
place.

PLATE 50   The moon over the sea at Napier

PICTURE ACKNOWLEDGMENTS

PLATES: 17 (top) Martin Barribal; Jacket pictures, 6, 8, 31, 36, 37, 49, K & J Bigwood; Frontispiece, 5 (two), 7 (lower), 9 (lower), 12, 13 (top), 14 (two), 18 (lower), 19 (two) 20 (two), 21 (top), 22 (two), 26, 28 (lower), 29, 30 (two), 32, (top), 34 (two), 38 (four), 39 (top), 40 (two), 43, 50, Catherine Contos; 16 (top), 39 (lower), C. F. Leete; 10, Miriam Macgregor; 18 (top), Derry McLauchlan; 1, National Publicity Studios; 2 (lower), N. Z. Aerial Mapping; 4, 13 (lower), 21 (lower), 23 (lower), 28 (top), 32 (lower), 33 (lower), M. C. Palmer; 3, 33 (top), 48, Fritz Prenzel; 7 (top), 9 (top), 23 (top), 44 (two), D. W. Sinclair; 11 (two), 15 (two), 16 (lower), 24, 25, 27, 35 45 46, 47, Robert Wells; 2 (top), 17 (lower), 41 (two), 42, James White.

OTHER REED BOOKS

EARLY STATIONS OF HAWKE'S BAY   Miriam Macgregor

Another popular book by Miriam Macgregor this time concentrating on the founding and fortunes of the first great sheep stations. A valuable source of reference, it includes seven short biographies of the women who helped pioneer the new land with their men folk.

HISTORIC SHEEP STATIONS OF THE NORTH ISLAND   Colin Wheeler

With his sketchpad, his oils and his biro, Colin Wheeler has recorded the special and distinctive features of twenty well-known northern stations, which he accompanies with an engaging text on the people and terrain of the stations.

INHERITORS OF A DREAM   Dick Scott

A pictorial presentation of New Zealand's social and economic progress from the early days of the pioneers to the present. More than 300 photographs, maps and drawings have been used to illuminate the country's development, and combined with the perceptive text, creates a unique picture of New Zealand.

TUTIRA   H. Guthrie-Smith

"'Tutira' has an honoured place among the very few first-class works that have come out of New Zealand.''—Encyclopaedia of New Zealand. In the author's 58 years on his sheep station in Hawke's Bay he witnessed astonishing changes in the station's ecology and plant and animal life, which he describes with remarkable lucidity, understanding and humour.

BIG COUNTRY OF THE NORTH ISLAND   Peter Newton

A survey of forty-five prominent stations in the eastern North Island region. Blended with the history of each station and anecdotes of New Zealand country life, is an account of its current size and potential.

MAORI HISTORY AND PLACE NAMES OF HAWKE'S BAY
J. D. H. Buchanan (editor D. R. Simmons)

An invaluable study of local Maori culture and a permanent record of people and place names that have been known—but not always located—since early times. As a practical guide it is unsurpassed.

HISTORIC TRAILS OF HAWKE'S BAY   Miriam Macgregor

A fascinating look at the early events and settlement patterns of the Bay, which also examines many historic landmarks and gives the stories behind them. Profusely illustrated.